Experiencing Easter

*The Lenten Journey
of Death to Life*

Gregory L. Tolle

CSS Publishing Company, Inc., Lima, Ohio

Scripture quotations are from the New Revised Standard Version of the Bible, copyright 1989 by the Division of Christian Education of the National Council of the Churches of Christ in the USA. Used by permission.

Library of Congress Cataloging-in-Publication Data

Tolle, Gregory L., 1966-
   Experiencing Easter : the Lenten journey of death to life / Greg Tolle.
     p. cm.
   ISBN 0-7880-2436-1 (perfect bound : alk. paper)
   1. Lenten sermons. 2. Sermons, American—21st century. 3. United Methodist Church (U.S.)—Sermons. I. Title.

   BV4277.T65 2007
   252'.62—dc22

                   2006032434

For more information about CSS Publishing Company resources, visit our website at www.csspub.com or email us at custserv@csspub.com or call (800) 241-4056.

Cover design by Nikki Nocera
ISBN-13: 979-0-7880-2436-7
ISBN-10: 0-7880-2436-1
                     PRINTED IN U.S.A.

This book is dedicated to the congregations at the First United Methodist Churches in Snyder, Oklahoma, and Mountain Park, Oklahoma, who endured the learning curve of a preacher direct from seminary, and to the congregation at FUMC Heavener, Oklahoma, who received a better preacher and released an even better one five years later. And, also, to my current church congregation, FUMC of Durant, Oklahoma, who benefits from the work of my previous churches and still challenges me to preach a better sermon.

Table Of Contents

Introduction

Easter is like the second to the last chapter of a book. It is the climax before the story is finally resolved in the final chapter. It is the point at which we want to arrive. There always seems to be those people who will read the first few chapters and then skip over to the last few so that they can get to the ending. And so it is with Easter. We want to arrive there on the fast track.

However, Lent is a process. So when this sermon series proposes experiencing Easter, it proposes to work through a process that struggles through Lent and then arrives in due time at our Easter destination. To truly experience Easter, we have to begin with the nature of humanity before discovering the nature of God. The gift of Easter has little meaning without an awareness of our need for redemption. Christ overcoming death does little for us if we don't understand the hold that death has over us.

Join in the journey that begins with the dirtiness of our lives, struggles through the wilderness, finds momentary hope, experiences defeat, then finally attains victory. Experience the fullness of Easter by taking this Lenten journey.

Have mercy on me, O God, according to your steadfast love; according to your abundant mercy blot out my transgressions. Wash me thoroughly from my iniquity, and cleanse me from my sin.

For I know my transgressions, and my sin is ever before me. Against you, you alone, have I sinned, and done what is evil in your sight, so that you are justified in your sentence and blameless when you pass judgment. Indeed, I was born guilty, a sinner when my mother conceived me.

You desire truth in the inward being; therefore teach me wisdom in my secret heart. Purge me with hyssop, and I shall be clean; wash me, and I shall be whiter than snow. Let me hear joy and gladness; let the bones that you have crushed rejoice. Hide your face from my sins, and blot out all my iniquities.

Create in me a clean heart, O God, and put a new and right spirit within me. Do not cast me away from your presence, and do not take your holy spirit from me. Restore to me the joy of your salvation, and sustain in me a willing spirit. — Psalm 51

Experiencing Clean Hearts

Last summer, my family went to Playa del Carmen, Mexico, for our vacation. Our trip included all transfers, which was a great benefit because it was a 45-minute drive to the nearest airport — Cancun.

We loaded onto the provided bus and let the children choose where to sit. They went to the back two rows. We then proceeded to the next resort to pick up other passengers also headed to the airport.

At the last resort, a particularly large group joined us. There were six adults and six to eight teenagers. They were spread out over the back half of the bus, taking up about four rows. It didn't take long to become annoyed by this group. They were loud as they yelled to each other so that the entire bus could hear. In fact, a family in the front seat later commented on this.

The loud group's conversations were sprinkled with profanities including using the name of Jesus in a non-prayerful way. They were lewd, rude, crude, and obnoxious. And it got worse as they all bought beer — including several of the teenagers who weren't legal in the US, but were legal in Mexico, so they were taking full advantage of it.

The loudest and most offensive was a mother who sat directly in front of me. Completely oblivious to the fact that my sleeping eight-year-old daughter and I were behind her, she fully reclined her seat, nearly crushing my foot in the process.

We devised a plan to quickly grab our bags once at the airport and put as much distance as possible between us and the loud, large group. This was hindered when the loud lady in front of me didn't put her seat back up, but we still accomplished the goal — kind of. Whereas most of the large group lingered while finding their luggage and smoking cigarettes, one couple went directly in the airport to the end of a lengthy line to check their luggage and receive their boarding passes — placing them directly in front of my family.

When the rest of the group arrived, they tried to reunite with the rest of their family, but fortunately were turned away by security.

However, they were still closer than I wanted them to be. Even though we had about twenty people separating us, they could still be heard over everyone else in line.

After getting our boarding passes, we were finally able to get away from the group. That is until we took a shuttle from the airport to the airplane. We boarded the shuttle first, but within minutes the loud people joined us. Of all the available space, they chose to stand next to us. The loud lady who invaded my space on the bus now bumped into my wife without any kind of acknowledgment or apology.

We let them off first and watched as they climbed the steps into the plane. At the top of the stairs, one of the teenage boys stopped, turned around, and waved good-bye to Mexico. He seemed to expect Mexico to respond, "We'll miss you. How will we ever live without you?"

I turned to my wife and said, "They seem to think that the entire world revolves around them!"

In truth, don't we all at times? Don't we sometimes get too full of ourselves and feel like we're "it"? Well, Ash Wednesday comes around to remind us that we are not. Instead, we are dust. Instead of being everything, we are nothing.

King David felt like he was everything, and why not? He has been called "a man after God's own heart." He was the king of Israel during the time of its greatest achievements. He was a poet laureate. He seemed to have everything and be everything.

Yet 2 Samuel, chapter 11, tells how David failed. He had an affair with Bathsheba and then succeeded in a plot to kill her husband after discovering she was pregnant. This was more than being lewd, rude, and crude on a bus — more than taking cuts in line at the airport. David broke half of the Ten Commandments. He coveted. He committed adultery. He murdered.

Second Samuel 11 also tells us that he was discovered. The prophet Nathan came to him and told an allegory to reveal David's sin. Even though David thought he was untouchable as the king of Israel, he was dust. His sin would separate him from God and lead to his death. Ashes to ashes. Dust to dust.

So how did David respond? He owned up to his actions. You get the feeling his sin haunted him, similar to the main character in Edgar Allan Poe's short story, *The Tell-Tale Heart*. In the story, the nameless narrator had committed murder and buried the dismembered body of his elderly victim beneath three planks of his floor.

He was poised to get away with his crime even as the police came to investigate. The murderer is unable to escape the haunting guilt of his deed. He began to hear the heartbeat of his dead victim. A cold sweat poured over him as the heartbeat relentlessly went on and on, getting louder and louder until the murderer confessed to his crime and showed the police the body.

Poe's point was that it was not the pounding heart of his victim that drove the man mad. Instead, it was pounding within his own chest. Even if he had committed the perfect murder, his guilt was too much to overcome. He was dust.

David's guilt drove him to a confession of sorts, but instead of going mad, he wrote poetic thoughts that we now know as Psalm 51. The rubrics of the psalm explain: "To the leader. A psalm of David, when the prophet Nathan came to him, after he had gone in to Bathsheba."

Psalm 51 is a prayer of pain. It is a prayer of failure as David uses terms like "transgressions," "iniquity," "guilty," "sinner," and "sin." When Nathan called David on his sin, he looked into his heart and didn't like what he saw. Who can blame him? When we look into our own hearts, are we comfortable with what we see?

A modern parable by an unknown author tells of six people gathered around a dying campfire on a dark and bitter night. Each one has a stick that could be placed on the fire. Sadly, one by one, they decide not to give what they have to keep the fire going.

The lone woman does not give because there is a black man in the circle. A penniless vagabond does not give because there is a member of the idle rich within the group. The rich man does not give because he reasons his contribution would obviously help someone who was lazy and shiftless. Another didn't give because one of the six didn't belong to his church. The black man hung tight to his wood, because it was his way of getting back at all the "whities." Still another would not give because he believed in giving only to those who also gave.

The parable ends with these words: "Six logs held fast in death's hand was proof of human sin, the sin of pride, ego, and selfishness. They didn't die from the cold of that night, the cold without; they died from the cold within each heart."

David knew his heart was not right. It was cold. It was selfish. He was living as if he was the only person that mattered. So he sought to change that about himself.

Psalm 51 is also a prayer of seeking God. David wrote, "Have mercy on me, O God, according to your steadfast love." He said, "Wash me" and "cleanse me" before uttering perhaps the most famous words of the psalm: "Create in me a clean heart, O God, and put a new and right spirit within me."

Not only does David confess his sin, but he also seeks to be cleansed of the very sin to which he confesses. Ash Wednesday is all about seeking a clean heart. Notice that David didn't say, "Change my behavior." He said, "Change my heart." He wants God to create him as a new person.

In 1992, professors Gloria Clayton and Leonard Poon published the results of an intensive study of centenarians — people who live to 100 years old, or more. One of the men they studied was Jesse Champion, 102 years old, who was active in his local church. In his interview, Mr. Champion said, "I know I've been born again." Then he added, "My hands look new. My feet look new. Yeah, he changed my heart. I had a hard heart, but he changed it."[1]

Can you imagine having a new heart at the age of 100? Yet, he felt his heart changed. This is what David was seeking from God. He wanted his heart changed. He wanted a clean heart. He wanted the sin that would lead to death to be out.

The verb "create" in verse 10 is *bara* in Hebrew and is used in the Old Testament only in context of what God does: such as in the creation stories of Genesis. David recognized God's fundamental character to restore, rehabilitate, and re-create sinners. David's life depended on God's willingness to forgive and to re-create sinners. So he called upon God to permeate his heart.

Ash Wednesday requires us to make the same request. It asks the question, "Have you let God penetrate your heart so that you can be re-created?"

In the movie *Godfather III*, Mafia boss, Michael Corleone, meets with Cardinal Lamberto and reports to the cardinal that executives from the Vatican bank and even an archbishop have been involved in a massive case of fraud. Upon hearing this news, Cardinal Lamberto moves to a water fountain, withdraws a stone, and says, "Look at this stone. It has been lying in the water for a very long time, but the water has not penetrated it."

He breaks the stone in two, shows the inside to the Mafia boss, and continues, "Look. Perfectly dry. The same thing has happened to men in Europe. For centuries they have been surrounded by Christianity, but Christ has not penetrated. Christ doesn't breathe within them."

Does Christ breathe within you? Lent is a journey to Easter — a journey to the resurrected Christ. That journey goes through the cross of Christ. Christ died so that we would not be condemned to dust — so that he could penetrate our cold, sinful, hardened hearts.

When the cross of ash is placed on our foreheads, it reminds us of two things: First, the ash reminds us who we are. We are dust. We are sinners with a death sentence. The world doesn't revolve around us. We are nothing.

However, even though the ash reminds us *who* we are, the cross reminds us *whose* we are. We belong to Christ. God through Christ provided a way for our hearts to be cleansed. God's Son, Jesus the Christ, was the embodiment of grace. In Christ, God clearly showed the willingness to rehabilitate the hearts of sinners.

In the story of David and Bathsheba, David's sinfulness does not have the last word. God's grace does. Sure, David's sin had serious consequences as his child born to Bathsheba died, and his family nearly fell apart, but David's sin was forgiven. He was allowed to live and to remain king.

As we begin our journey of experiencing Easter, let us honestly look at our hearts and acknowledge the dust that we are. Then, let us seek grace. May we allow God to cleanse us — to create a new and right spirit in our hearts. Amen.

---

1. Hugh Downs, *Fifty to Forever* (Nashville: T. N. Publishers, 1994), p. 65.

When you have come into the land that the Lord your God is giving you as an inheritance to possess, and you possess it, and settle in it, you shall take some of the first of all the fruit of the ground, which you harvest from the land that the Lord your God is giving you, and you shall put it in a basket and go to the place that the Lord your God will choose as a dwelling for his name. You shall go to the priest who is in office at that time, and say to him, "Today I declare to the Lord your God that I have come into the land that the Lord swore to our ancestors to give us." When the priest takes the basket from your hand and sets it down before the altar of the Lord your God, you shall make this response before the Lord your God: "A wandering Aramean was my ancestor; he went down into Egypt and lived there as an alien, few in number, and there he became a great nation, mighty and populous. When the Egyptians treated us harshly and afflicted us, by imposing hard labor on us, we cried to the Lord of our ancestors; the Lord heard our voice and saw our affliction, our toil, and our oppression. The Lord brought us out of Egypt with a mighty hand and an outstretched arm, with a terrifying display of power, and with signs and wonders; and he brought us into this place and gave us this land, a land flowing with milk and honey. So now I bring the first of the fruit of the ground that you, O Lord, have given me." You shall set it down before the Lord your God and bow down before the Lord your God. Then you, together with the Levites and the aliens who reside among you, shall celebrate with all the bounty that the Lord your God has given to you and to your house.   — Deuteronomy 26:1-11

Lent 1
Deuteronomy 26:1-11

Experiencing Wilderness

A woman was trying to impress everyone at a party with her heritage. She said, "My family's ancestry is very old. It dates back to the days of King James." She then turned to another woman who was quietly sitting in a corner and asked very condescendingly, "How old is your family, dear?"

The woman calmly answered, "I can't really say for sure. All our family records were lost in Noah's flood."

We take great pride in our heritage, don't we? It is a part of who we are. But as important as heritage is in creating who we are, there are other more important factors.

A few years ago, I attended Minister's Week at my alma mater — Brite Divinity School at Texas Christian University. Dr. Andy Lester presented a series of lectures on pastoral care for anger within the church. Dr. Lester's approach was built around what he termed "Narrative Theory."

In a nutshell, Narrative Theory is a belief that every person has events in their past that affect their present and their future. In the case of his lectures, anger was caused by past events. But Narrative Theory deals with more than just anger — more than just negative events. All significant events are a part of our story. These stories help create us. They make us who we are. When we don't know our past, we are like amnesiacs; we've lost our identity. It's like we are in a wilderness, not knowing our way.

In today's scripture passage from Deuteronomy, Moses summarizes the story of the Hebrew people. While advising the people to be generous to God, he reminds them of their heritage by reciting an early creed — like an ancient Hebrew Apostles' Creed. The creed recalled their history and heritage:

19

A wandering Aramean was my ancestor; he went down into Egypt and lived there as an alien, few in number, and there he became a great nation, mighty and populous. When the Egyptians treated us harshly and afflicted us, by imposing hard labor on us, we cried to the Lord, the God of our ancestors; the Lord heard our voice and saw our affliction, our toil, and our oppression. The Lord brought us out of Egypt with a mighty hand and an outstretched arm, with a terrifying display of power, and with signs and wonders; and he brought us into this place and gave us this land, a land flowing with milk and honey.

— Deuteronomy 26:5b-9

Their story began with "a wandering Aramean" which was a reminder that their forefather was homeless and jobless. That would be Jacob, son of Isaac, son of Abraham. Jacob is the result of God's promise that Abraham would produce a great nation. The people grew great in Egypt before eventually becoming enslaved. Then God provided Moses to lead them out. But before arriving at the land of milk and honey, they spent forty years in the wilderness.

That story is our story as well. These are our ancestors, and this is our history. Like our ancestors, we find ourselves enslaved at times and wandering aimlessly in the wilderness. This is a part of the Lenten journey — a recognition that we are enslaved to sin and that we wander in the wilderness in our attempt to make our way to the promised land.

We sometimes have the misconception that there is no wilderness within the Christian journey. We mistakenly believe that it will be all promised land and no wilderness. The truth is that the wilderness is a part of the journey. The promise is that God will guide us through the wilderness if we will trust God to guide us out.

This is the good news. God calls us out of the wilderness. At those times that we are lost and wandering aimlessly in life, God will provide guidance to the promised land.

Charisma magazine reported of such a wilderness coming out event. Three men from California were traveling to the Promise Keepers' "Stand in the Gap" rally in Washington DC, back in

October 1997. While driving to the event, they passed a homeless man on their way out of town. They stopped and invited him to go with them. The man responded that he wasn't worthy of attending the event. He had left his family in Alabama sixteen years prior and hadn't seen them since.

The men explained that while they hadn't physically abandoned their families, they had failed in other ways. The purpose of the event was to repent for these failures and reconcile. This convinced the man to go.

As they arrived at the capital, the three Promise Keepers told the man that they would try to find a group from Alabama so he could talk to someone from his home state. Standing in the midst of one million men, the task seemed impossible, but the first group they met was from Alabama.

As the homeless man talked with the group from Alabama, he discovered one of the men was from his hometown. The two men then introduced themselves and discovered that they knew each other. The homeless man had just re-met the son he had abandoned sixteen years before. The two spent the day reconciling and praying together, then both returned home to Alabama.[1]

Talk about wilderness. This homeless man was like a wandering Aramean. And you can bet his son felt like he was in the wilderness for the past sixteen years. And yet both show their trust in God as they were seeking God through the Promise Keepers' event.

Does this story sound too incredible to be true? Some may think so — just as people have been skeptical of God's intervention in the lives of biblical people.

But verse 8 reminds us that God leads us "with a mighty hand ... with terrifying display of power, and with signs and wonders." Think for a moment on the mighty and powerful signs of the exodus: plagues upon plagues and the parting of the Reed Sea. If God has the power for all that, can't God miraculously bring a man and his son out of the wilderness?

Unbelievable? Not to people of faith. To believers, the exodus story and the homeless man's story are incredible only in the amount of God's love displayed. They are a witness of God working in the midst of our painful lives.

There are countless stories of God's love and intercession in the wilderness of our lives. Renowned optimist, Zig Zigler, tells of one story connected with the classic movie *Gone with the Wind* and its more recent sequel, *Scarlett*. Sure we're all familiar with the story, but how many of us know that these tales of Rhett Butler and Scarlett O'Hara were loosely based on a true story?

Rhett's actual last name was Turnipseed and Scarlett was really Emelyn Louise Hannon. (Chalk one up for poetic license.) And, as portrayed in the movie, Rhett did walk out on her to join the Confederate Army. When the war was over, Rhett Turnipseed entered the wilderness as he became a drifter and a gambler. He ended up in Nashville where his life was turned around. On Easter morning in 1871, he attended a Methodist revival meeting and became a committed Christian.

Soon afterward, Rhett enrolled at Vanderbilt University and became a Methodist preacher. While a preacher, a young woman in his church ran away to St. Louis and became a prostitute. Rhett was concerned about her and rode to St. Louis to look for her. He found her at a house of ill repute where the madam was none other than Emelyn Louise Hannon — the real Scarlett.

Emelyn refused to let Rhett see the young woman. So Rhett challenged her to a game of cards. If he won, the girl went free. If Emelyn won, the girl remained. Rhett won.

Actually, everyone won. The young girl eventually married and became a matriarch of an important family in Tennessee. Emelyn became so impressed with Rhett's transformation that she, too, became a Christian. Eventually, she opened a Methodist orphanage for Cherokee children.[2]

Just one more story of how God led people out of the wilderness and into the promised land. When we stop and reflect on life, we all have times that we have come out of the wilderness — a story of how God has been a part of our life when we were wandering aimlessly.

It probably isn't as dramatic as those we've heard this morning. Most of us haven't been a compulsive gambler, a prostitute, a madam, a homeless person, or a slave in the land of Egypt. But we still have our story — the story of how we've experienced God's love in the midst of painful times. We all have encountered hardships — low points, but we can also recall how God pulled us through.

If we have not been slaves in Egypt, we have still been enslaved to sin.

If we have not been homeless, we have still had times when home was less than perfect.

If we have not been a prostitute, a madam, or a gambler, we have still compromised our ethics and taken what looked liked the easy way out.

Deuteronomy 26:7 says, "We cried to the Lord ... the Lord heard our voice and saw our affliction." This is a reminder of the good news: God hears our cries and sees our pain. This is why God wants to have a relationship with us — to bring us out of the wilderness. To heal our pain and comfort our cries.

We have our wilderness-to-promised land story. True to Narrative Theory, those events have shaped us — helped make us who we are. But what should we do with our story?

First, we remember our story and give thanks to God for the blessings we have been given. We have been led from the wilderness to the promised land. Lent is a wonderful time to reflect on where we've been and where we are going.

And secondly, consider how our story connects with *the* story. How does our entrance into the promised land connect with our entrance into the kingdom of God? Our story connects with tradition — from Adam to the second Adam, known to us as Jesus Christ. Go back to wondrous story of scripture — particularly the gospel of salvation. Read. Pray. Listen.

And then as we understand our testimony in light of the testament of Christ, we should repeat our story like a creed. Our story of God's gift of deliverance creates an opportunity for us to help and encourage others when they are in the wilderness. Just as Rhett Turnipseed's testimony and the homeless man's witness show the power and love of God, so does our story. You might think it is blasé, but it just might be the word somebody needs to hear — and the only way they can hear the gospel.

So what's your story? Whatever it is, I praise God for the great things done in your life. I thank God for however you have been brought and nourished into Christian fellowship. Remember your story — it is a part of who you are. Remember the gospel story, then share the story of deliverance! Amen.

---

1. http://www.goodnewsmag.org/.

2. Zig Zigler, *Something to Smile About* (Nashville, Tennessee: Thomas Nelson, Inc., 1997), pp. 55-56.

The Lord is my light and my salvation; whom shall I fear? The Lord is the stronghold of my life; of whom shall I be afraid?

When evildoers assail me to devour my flesh — my adversaries and foes — they shall stumble and fall.

Though an army encamp against me, my heart shall not fear; though war rise up against me, yet I will be confident.

One thing I asked of the Lord, that will I seek after: to live in the house of the Lord all the days of my life, to behold the beauty of the Lord, and to inquire in his temple.

For he will hide me in his shelter in the day of trouble; he will conceal me under the cover of his tent; he will set me high on a rock.

Now my head is lifted up above my enemies all around me, and I will offer in his tent sacrifices with shouts of joy; I will sing and make melody to the Lord.

Hear, O Lord, when I cry aloud, be gracious to me and answer me! "Come," my heart says, "see, his face!" Your face, Lord, do I seek. Do not hide your face from me.

Do not turn your servant away in anger, you who have been my help. Do not cast me off, do not forsake me, O God of my salvation! If my father and mother forsake me, the Lord will take me up.

Teach me your way, O Lord, and lead me on a level path because of my enemies. Do not give me up to the will of my adversaries, for false witnesses have risen against me, and they are breathing out violence.

I believe that I shall see the goodness of the Lord in the land of the living. Wait for the Lord; be strong, and let your heart take courage; wait for the Lord!

— Psalm 27

Experiencing Fearlessness

A hospital administrator was startled to see a patient fleeing down the hall out of the operating room — his loose gown flapping in the breeze. He stopped the patient and asked why he was running from the operating room. The patient said, "Because of what the nurse said."

The administrator queried, "Well, what did she say?"

The patient reported, "She said, 'Be brave. An appendectomy is quite simple.'"

The administrator replied, "What's the big deal? I would think that would comfort you."

The patient explained, "She said it to the doctor!"

Fear ... it can be an incredible motivator — and an incredible deterrent. A sergeant in a parachute regiment took part in several nighttime exercises. Once, he was seated next to a lieutenant fresh from jump school. He was quite sad and looked a bit pale, so the sergeant struck up a conversation. He asked, "Scared, Lieutenant?"

The lieutenant replied, "No, just a bit apprehensive."

The sergeant asked, "What's the difference?"

He replied, "That means I'm scared with a college education."

Fear is something to be conquered. The catchphrase embraced a few years ago by Generation X was simply put: "No Fear." That motto has been lived out by the daredevilish X Games — in sports like bungee jumping, snowboarding, and mountain biking.

It also has been lived out on television with the show, *Fear Factor* — part reality show, part game show, and pretty much all disgusting. People eat live insects or perform dangerous stunts for a chance to win $50,000. As repulsive as it is, the focus of the show is people facing their fears. And Gen Xers line up to show that they are fearless.

In today's scripture, the psalmist writes that he has experienced fearlessness. He is surviving threats against his very life. In the first verse, he says, "The Lord is my light and my salvation; whom shall I fear? The Lord is the stronghold of my life; of whom shall I be afraid?" And he adds in verse 3, "my heart shall not fear."

But unlike *Fear Factor* contestants, the psalmist clearly identifies why he has experienced fearlessness. His source for relieving fear — his source for survival — is God. His faith in God took away his fear even as his enemies confronted him.

The psalmist expresses this by referring to God as "my light." He has a belief that no matter how dark life may seem — including the threat of death — God would be there as a light shining in the darkness.

Years ago, a little girl rode a train with her family. At night they slept in the sleeping car and the little girl slept on the top bunk by herself. Mom assured her that they would be right below her and God would look after her.

With the darkness came quietness. The little girl became scared. She called out, "Mommy, are you there?"

Her mother replied, "Yes, dear, and remember God will look after you."

A few minutes passed and she asked her father the same question. Her dad assured her that he was right below her. Several minutes later, the questions were repeated and she also asked about her brother and her sister. Each "yes" quieted her — for a while.

Later when she started asking the same question again, another passenger lost his patience. In a deep voice he said, "We're all here. Your father, your mother, your brother, and your sister. Now, go to sleep!"

There was complete silence. Then the little girl whispered, "Mommy, was that God?"[1]

The little girl expressed her belief that God cared enough to be with her in the darkness. Darkness held nothing over her — God was there to calm her fears. She believed what her mother told her — God would look after her. She believed that God was her light in the midst of the darkness.

But God is more than just light. The psalmist also referred to God as *my salvation*, which in biblical terms means *life*. In the midst of death and darkness, God is life — the Creator and giver of life saves us.

When the Golden Gate Bridge of San Francisco was being built, workers developed a great fear of falling to their deaths. Can you blame them? The impact of falling from the bridge to the water is the equivalent of hitting a brick wall at eighty miles per hour.

Bridge builders used to have a superstition that one man would die for every million dollars spent on a project. Since the bridge had a $35 million budget, the workers feared a loss of three dozen men. Fear became reality in the early days of the project: some twenty workers died or were seriously injured when they fell into San Francisco Bay.

Finally, construction was stopped, and chief engineer, Joseph Strauss, made an unprecedented move. He ordered a large trapeze net to be installed under the work area.

Over the next several years, only four men fell off the bridge. Not only did the net make work conditions safer — but it also made workers feel more confident and less likely to fall. As one worker put it, the added security made them feel as though they could "dance on the steel." The net changed their entire outlook.[2]

That is the kind of faith we can have in God. No matter what is going on around us, we can have confidence that God will save us — God is our safety net in life. In the face of danger, we can experience fearlessness.

The psalmist also refers to God as a *stronghold* and a *tent*. He believes in a strong, personal, and loving God who will shelter him and hide him from harm — much like a parent protects a child.

One tribe of Native Americans had a unique practice for training young braves. On the night of a boy's thirteenth birthday, he was placed in a dense forest to spend the entire night alone. Until then, he had never been away from the security of his family and tribe. But on this night, he was blindfolded and taken miles away. When he took off the blindfold, he was in the middle of thick woods — by himself — all night long.

Every time a twig snapped, he probably visualized a wild animal ready to pounce. Every time an animal howled, he imagined a wolf leaping out of the darkness. Every time the wind blew, he wondered what more sinister sound it masked. No doubt it was a terrifying night for many.

After what seemed like an eternity, the first rays of sunlight entered the interior of the forest. Looking around, the boy saw flowers, trees, and the outline of the path. Then, to his astonishment he beheld the figure of a man standing just a few feet away, armed with a bow and arrow. It was the boy's father. He had been there all night long.[3]

In verse 5, the psalmist writes, "For he will hide me in his shelter in the day of trouble; he will conceal me under the cover of his tent." We need to strive for the same kind of faith that believes God is present with us — a few feet away. That God is our light in the darkness, our salvation, and our protector.

Our time has been called the "age of anxiety," which makes the psalmist's example of faith all the more important. Psalm 27 suggests that the opposite of faith is not doubt — but fear. If we don't believe in God — and trust in God — then there is a persistent anxiety in life.

But, if we do believe and trust in God as our light, salvation, and protector, we can be fearless. We have no reason to be anxious and afraid. To borrow from Franklin Delano Roosevelt's inaugural address, "The only thing we have to fear is fear itself."

And fear should be feared if it keeps us from faith. Only fear keeps us from standing on the stronghold of God. Fear is not a failure of nerve — it is a failure of trust. Fear can cause us to trust ourselves instead of placing our lives in God's hands. It takes faith to trust God. But we sometimes abandon that faith when things get uncomfortable and we turn back to trusting self.

Two men were assigned to stand watch on a ship out at sea. During the night, the waves from a raging storm washed one of them overboard. The sailor who drowned had been in the most sheltered place, while the one who survived was more exposed to the elements. What made the difference? The man who had been lost had nothing to hold on to.

What a picture of the way some people are affected by the trials of life! When life is peaceful, they seem very self-sufficient, but when the going gets rough they are swept off their feet. Because they have not believed in God and not trusted God, they have nothing to hold on to, so they are easily overwhelmed. Left to depend on ourselves instead of on God, we fail to experience joy (v. 6) and life in all its fullness (v. 13).

Christians, who trust and cling to God as our light, salvation, and protector, can weather the fiercest storms of adversity. This is the promise of Psalm 27 — God will be our stronghold. We can cling to God. Little test and trials expose us to the elements. They turn us to God so that we may be hid "in his shelter in the day of trouble." What a great promise! We can trust God and God will see us through.

James S. Hewett writes of growing up in Pennsylvania. As a small boy, his family would often visit his grandparents who lived nine miles away. One night, a thick fog settled over the hilly countryside before they started home. Hewett was terrified, and asked if they shouldn't be going even slower than they were. His mother said gently, "Don't worry. Your father knows the way."

You see, his father had walked that road during the war when there was no gasoline. He had ridden that blacktop on his bicycle to court James' mother. And for years he had made those weekly trips back to visit his own parents.

Hewett writes, "How often when I can't see the road of life, and have felt that familiar panic rising in my heart I have heard the echo of my mother's voice. 'Don't worry. Your Father knows the way.' "[4]

God knows the way — and we are protected in God's care if we will only trust in God. If we believe in God, our fear can be resolved.

Psalm 27 talks about the "evildoers" who "devour your flesh." We all face people in life who are cruel and situations that seem overwhelming. But Psalm 27 reminds us not to have fear, but to have faith.

God loves us. God is our light, our refuge, and our stronghold. We survive because God shelters us. No fear. Just faith. Experience the fearlessness that comes with trusting God! Amen.

---

1. *Bits & Pieces* magazine (Chicago: Ragan's Motivational Resources), 3/5/92, pp. 21-22.

2. Raymond McHenry, *The Best of In Other Words* (self-published, 1996), p. 223.

3. Leonard Sweet, *Soulsalsa* (Grand Rapids, Michigan: Zondervan Bible Publishers, 2002), pp. 23-24.

4. James Hewett, *Illustrations Unlimited* (Wheaton: Tyndale House Publishers, 1988), p. 201.

At that very time there were some present who told him about the Galileans whose blood Pilate had mingled with their sacrifices. He asked them, "Do you think that because these Galileans suffered in this way they were worse sinners than all other Galileans? No, I tell you; but unless you repent, you will all perish as they did. Or those eighteen who were killed when the tower of Siloam fell on them — do you think that they were worse offenders than all the others living in Jerusalem? No, I tell you; but unless you repent, you will all perish just as they did."

Then he told this parable: "A man had a fig tree planted in his vineyard; and he came looking for fruit on it and found none. So he said to the gardener, 'See here! For three years I have come looking for fruit on this fig tree, and still I find none. Cut it down! Why should it be wasting the soil?' He replied, 'Sir, let it alone for one more year, until I dig round it and put manure on it. If it bears fruit next year, well and good; but if not, you can cut it down.' "   — Luke 13:1-9

Experiencing Second Chances

Why is it that if someone says there are a billion stars out, we never question the accuracy? But if there is a sign that says "Wet Paint," we just have to touch it to see if it's true?

Why is it that we drive on parkways and park on driveways? And why do we call a road a "highway" when it is on ground level?

Why is it that when someone says, "A penny for your thoughts," we never get paid? Instead, we insist on getting in "our two-cents worth" and then never pay anyone to listen to us. And shouldn't have inflation changed the going rate of thoughts by now?

Some questions are simply not intended to be answered. Some are irrelevant or not worth the time to ponder — like the ones I've already asked, but others are beyond our knowledge — too tough to answer. If you could ask God one question, you wouldn't waste it on something fluffy and frivolous. Instead, wouldn't you search the depths of your soul and find a deep, philosophical question?

The little book, *Children's Letters to God*, is filled with deep theological questions as asked by children — in the form of letters to God. Children are so inquisitive and completely uninhibited in asking. They ask questions that we adults haven't wrestled with in some time. They openly ponder the great mysteries of the universe. Well, at least mysteries in their world.

Lucy asks, "Are you really invisible or is that just a trick?"

Nan wonders, "Who draws the lines around the countries?"

Nell says, "I went to this wedding and they kissed right in church. Is that okay?"

And Jane inquires, "Instead of letting people die and making new ones, why not keep the ones you got now?"[1]

Good question. It's one we all ask in various ways. Why do people die? Why is there suffering? Why do bad things happen to good people? Are bad things caused by our sins and failures?

In the movie, *Oh, God, Book II*, God, portrayed by George Burns, is asked by a little girl why bad things happen. Burns replies, "That's the way the system works. Have you ever seen an up, without a down? A front, without a back? A top, without a bottom? You can't have one without the other. If I take away sad, then I take away happy, too. They go together."

Then Burns adds with a smile, "If somebody has a better idea, I hope they put it in the suggestion box."[2]

Obviously, none of the *Oh, God* movies were meant to be great theological works. But the movie shows that we have more questions than we do answers in life. Part of the reason for that is because we can't stand face-to-face with God like in *Oh, God* and have our questions directly answered. We can't exactly write a letter to God and receive a written reply.

In today's scripture lesson when Jesus is asked similar questions about suffering, he doesn't directly deal with the "why." This is the scenario: Apparently as the crowd was listening to Jesus teach, they were also passing along the news of a recent religiously related "hate crime." Pilate's soldiers had murdered some Galilean Jews while they were offering sacrifices. The fact that human blood was mixed with animal blood in the slaughter made the deaths all the worse. Mixing blood was atrocious in Jewish culture.

The crowd wondered why these Galileans had to suffer in such a way. Then they tried to answer their own question. They assumed that such a horrible and disgraceful death could only mean one thing. These Galileans were major sinners who deserved God's wrath and punishment.

Jesus makes one thing perfectly clear to the crowd. They were wrong. Their belief simply is not true. God does not harm people as punishment. Jesus even recalls a tragic accident in Jerusalem where a wall near the pool of Siloam fell and crushed eighteen people. By doing so, Jesus essentially says, "Accidents happen and people are evil of their own free will, but God does not send calamities to punish people."

Jesus' response also says we're asking the wrong question. We're worried about the wrong things. We shouldn't wonder about the cause of the calamity. Instead, we should use the tragedy as a wake-up call to repent and draw closer to God. Life is fragile, and any of us could stand before our Maker in a moment's notice. Trials and tragedies are reminders that we have another chance to make up with God after we have failed in the human-divine relationship.

Twice in the scripture, Jesus calls us to "repent" which literally means "to turn around" or "to turn your back." When Jesus calls for us to repent, he means that we turn around from the wrong way and turn our back on sin. This is not a minor change, but a transformation of character.

When my children hurt or offend each other, they have to say "I'm sorry." But often their words are not heartfelt. So, we tell them, "I'm sorry" means that they will do their absolute very best to not repeat the mistake. That should be their intentions when they say "I'm sorry" to someone.

In simple terms, that's what repentance means. We will do our absolute very best to stop offending God — to stop our failure. We intend to end our sinful ways and to better live within God's will. We stop running away from God and start running to God.

At 33, Gary Hawkins had lived outside God's will. He had a fast, hard life filled with drugs, parties, and sexual promiscuity. But his life changed with a visit to his doctor and a discovery that he was HIV positive. He had no signs of sickness, but the virus lay dormant in his system.

With the news, Gary crashed.

He moved in with his parents and did little else other than watch television, eat pizza, and drink beer. He would die of AIDS, so why should he take care of himself? He sunk deeper and deeper into depression until he rarely left the house.

Finally, Gary's father had enough. He couldn't stand to see his son stop living before he died. Gary's father started leaving him "to-do lists" — things like shopping and cleaning. He also took away Gary's car keys and gave him a bike for transportation.

Tough love — but Gary gradually began to reenter the world. By riding his bike, he starting shaping up — both physically and mentally. He started swimming, jogging, and eating right. After six months, he entered his first triathlon.

On a visit to his doctor before the race, Gary received some good news. There was almost no trace of HIV in his system. His doctor cautioned him that he was not cured, but it was amazing that hardly any trace of the virus could be found in his blood.

Gary had a complete turnaround. First, he turned his back on partying and then he turned his back on giving up on life. He was on a path to destruction, but he turned around and took a path to wholeness and healing.[3]

God wants a better and healthier life for us. This is why Jesus balances the warnings of God's judgment with promises of God's mercy. There is an opportunity to experience second chances. He tells the parable of the fig tree to say that God would even give a fig tree a second chance. A fig tree normally takes three years to reach maturity. If it does not produce fruit by that time, it is not likely to produce fruit at all. But this fig tree was given another chance. If God would give a fig tree the gift of another year of life, then God will give us the same chance to bear fruit.

Dennis Becker is pastor of Faith Lutheran Church in Oshawa, Ontario. He was coaching his daughter's softball team when he had the unenviable task of having to cut a young lady from the team. Brenda couldn't hit, catch fly balls, or run the bases. Cutting her would simply save Brenda a lot of wasted time.

During the final practice before the team was announced, Becker's daughter suggested he try Brenda at first base. The two had played catch and Brenda caught everything thrown her way — even the wild ones.

Becker was skeptical, but tried her anyway. It was her last chance to make the team. He was pleasantly surprised. She struggled with the fly balls, but could catch all the infield throws. As the season progressed, Brenda's confidence grew and she improved on catching the fly balls. If Becker's daughter hadn't recognized Brenda's potential, she wouldn't have made the cut.[4]

In the same way Becker's daughter interceded for a second chance for Brenda, God's Son intercedes for a second chance for us — to show our potential. To repent and bear fruit. Through Jesus Christ, God keeps on forgiving us.

One rainy afternoon, a woman was driving along one of the main streets of town. Suddenly, her seven-year-old son, Matthew, spoke up: "Mom, I'm thinking of something."

She eagerly asked, "What are you thinking?"

He said, "The rain is like sin and the windshield wipers are like God, wiping our sins away."

Chill bumps raced up her arms at his innocent wisdom, in awe she replied, "That's really good, Matthew." Her curiosity pushed her to press his revelation. She asked, "Do you notice how the rain keeps on coming? What does that tell you?"

Matthew didn't hesitate a moment to answer, "We keep on sinning, and God just keeps on forgiving us."

Isn't it comforting to know that God shows mercy and keeps offering forgiveness? Within our humanity, we continue to sin. We may move beyond one form of sin only to discover a new failure, but God is standing ready to forgive us of that, as well. We continue to repent, and God continues to forgive. We continue to turn our back on sin while turning toward God, and God continues to wash our sins away.

Imagine that you had only one year left to live. You had only a short time to make up for wrong doings, failures, and missed opportunities. How important that year would be! The lesson of the fig tree is a challenge to live each day as a gift from God.

We have no need to ask God why bad things happen. Or even why we have been kept from tragedy. Instead we should take the tragedy as a reminder of the gift God has given us. We have a gift of time to repent — to turn away from evil and turn back to God. We have the gift of forgiveness once we repent.

Lent reminds us that even in the midst of our failures, God has given us an opportunity to experience a second chance. What we do with that opportunity is up to us. May we celebrate that gift by continuing to seek to grow as individuals and as Christians. May we live as changed and forgiven people. Amen.

1. Stuart Hample and Eric Marshall, *Children's Letters to God* (New York: Workman Publishing Co., 1991).

2. Tim Hansel, *Keep On Dancing* (Colorado Springs: Cook Communications Ministries, 1995), p. 43.

3. *Emphasis* (Lima, Ohio: CSS Publishing Company, Inc., 2001), March-April issue, p. 31.

4. *Ibid.*

Now all the tax collectors and sinners were coming near to listen to him. And the Pharisees and the scribes were grumbling and saying, "This fellow welcomes sinners and eats with them."

So he told them this parable:

Then Jesus said, "There was a man who had two sons. The younger of them said to his father, 'Father, give me the share of the property that will belong to me.' So he divided his property between them. A few days later the younger son gathered all he had and traveled to a distant country, and there he squandered his property in dissolute living. When he had spent everything, a severe famine took place throughout that country, and he began to be in need. So he went and hired himself out to one of the citizens of that country, who sent him to his fields to feed the pigs. He would gladly have filled himself with the pods that the pigs were eating; and no one gave him anything. But when he came to himself he said, 'How many of my father's hired hands have bread enough and to spare, but here I am dying of hunger! I will get up and go to my father, and I will say to him, "Father, I have sinned against heaven and before you; I am no longer worthy to be called your son; treat me like one of your hired hands." ' So he set off and went to his father. But while he was still far off, his father saw him and was filled with compassion; he ran and put his arms around him and kissed him. Then the son said to him, 'Father, I have sinned against heaven and before you; I am no longer worthy to be called your son.' But the father said to his slaves, 'Quickly, bring out a robe — the best one — and put it on him; put a ring on his finger and sandals on his feet. And get the fatted calf and kill it, and let us eat and celebrate; for this son of mine was dead and is alive again; he was lost and is found!' And they began to celebrate."

— Luke 15:1-3, 11b-24

Lent 4
Luke 15:1-3, 11b-24

Experiencing Forgiveness

A seminary professor taught the Christian graces of love and forgiveness for forty years until he retired. Now in retirement, he began working on delayed home improvement projects. First, he poured a new concrete driveway to his house. While the concrete set, he went to his kitchen for a glass of iced tea. Upon returning later to view his proud achievement, he discovered that the neighborhood kids were putting their footprints in the wet concrete. In a rage, the angry professor chased the kids down the street yelling at them in a very un-Christian manner.

Hearing the commotion, the professor's wife rushed into the yard, saw her husband's tirade, and began to reprimand him. She said, "What a shame! For forty years you have taught love, forgiveness, and self-control. Now look at you. You've lost your testimony."

To which he replied, "That was all in the abstract. This is in the concrete."

A groaner, I know, but the point is valid. Living out love and forgiveness requires more than theory. It requires practice. Jesus modeled it with his life. That is the gospel story. He also illustrated it with the parable that is today's scripture passage.

In the story Jesus told of a man who had two sons. He apparently was a wealthy Jewish landowner. His youngest son was somewhat of a rebel. By law, the youngest son would inherit one-third of the family property. When he was old enough, he asked his father for his portion of the inheritance. This was an outrageous breech of family protocol. But then he sold the property, which publicized the family problems, bringing shame to the father.

The son promptly left home and ventured into exotic foreign lands where he blew it all in a partying lifestyle. The sins of youth.

It reminds me of a true story told by Brady Whitehead, chaplain of Lambuth College in Tennessee. A student's parents were tragically killed in an accident and the student suddenly became the beneficiary of the estate. According to Brady, he started squandering the money on lavish trips. He would even invite other students to go along at his expense.

He was spending the money so fast that Brady called him into his office one day and had a talk with him. He said that as chaplain of the school he felt it was his responsibility to question his spending habits. The student responded: "But what you don't understand is just how much money I have inherited." "Well, that may be so," said Brady, "but even to a large estate there comes an end."

The student did not listen, and Brady revealed that by the time he graduated from Lambuth, all of his parents' money was gone.

And sure enough, in the scripture, the boy's money ran out.

He discovered he had no friends without his money. A famine hit the land and the only job he could find was slopping hogs. The pay was poor and the working conditions were terrible. More importantly, hogs were detestable to Jews.

One day he was so hungry and so despondent that he came to his senses, realizing that even the hired hands on his father's farm received better treatment than what he was experiencing on the hog farm. He quit his job and started for home. He was broken, humbled, and he wanted his father to take him back — but not as a son — this time, just as one of the farm hands.

It is at this point of the story that we start to get a glimpse of God's overwhelming forgiveness. We commonly call this teaching of Jesus "the parable of the prodigal son." It's a mistake because the son is not the hero. Instead, it should be called "the parable of the loving father," for the point is the father's love rather than the son's sin.

In verse 20, Jesus says, "But while he was still far off, his father saw him and was filled with compassion; he ran and put his arms around him and kissed him."

The fact that the father saw his son while he was way off in the distance means he was looking for his son. The father must have been waiting and watching for the son to come home. And as soon as he knew his son was taking steps to come home, he ran, which was completely undignified. This tells us that God can't wait to have us back when we have strayed.

David Redding, in his book, *Jesus Makes Me Laugh With Him*, tells a story about Teddy, his big, black, Scottish shepherd dog. Teddy would do anything for Redding. The dog waited for him to come home from school and slept beside him. Teddy worked with Redding in the fields from sunup to sundown. When Redding whistled, Teddy would even stop eating to run to him. At night, no one would get within a half mile of the house without Teddy's permission. When Redding went off to war, the one he hated telling the most was Teddy.

When Redding returned home from the Navy, he had to walk fourteen miles to the farm from the bus stop. He started walking about eleven o'clock at night and it was two or three in the morning before he was within a half mile of the house. It was pitch dark, but he knew every step of the way.

Suddenly, Teddy heard him and began his warning barking. Then Redding whistled only once. The barking stopped. There was a yelp of recognition. Almost immediately, the big black dog was in his arms.

Redding writes:

> To this day, that is the best way I can explain what I mean by coming home. What comes home to me now is the eloquence with which that unforgettable memory speaks to me of God. If my dog, without any explanation, would love me and take me back after all that time, would not my God?[1]

Let me tell you, no matter how far you strayed away from the faith, no matter what your past was like, God sees you and wants you back in the family. Rodney Dangerfield quipped, "Once when I was lost, I saw a policeman and asked him to help me find my parents. I said to him, 'Do you think we'll ever find them?' He said, 'I don't know, kid. There are so many places they can hide.'"

Isn't it great that God doesn't see it that way? When we are lost in life, God doesn't hide. God waits for our return — searching the horizon for our shadowy figure. D. L. Moody put it well: "The prodigal's father was looking through the telescope of his love."

We see this through the father's kiss. Notice, he didn't wait until the boy's clothes had been changed from the hog-smelling rags he had on. He also didn't wait until the hog waste was washed off his son's feet and hands. In just the state he was in, the father threw his arms around the boy and drew him close to his heart, and gave him a kiss — which was the sign of complete reconciliation. The father completely forgave the son before the son could even apologize. His sin was forgotten.

Once, Abraham Lincoln was asked how he was going to treat the rebellious southerners when they had finally been defeated and had returned to the union of the United States. The questioner expected that Lincoln would take a position of vengeance, but he answered, "I will treat them as if they had never been away."

That's God's position when we have strayed and run away. If we are willing to come back, then God is willing to forgive. Think about it in relationship to an Etch-A-Sketch™. I'm sure most of us have played with one. You can draw and draw and draw on one. And when you make a mistake or when you just don't like what you've drawn, you just shake the Etch-A-Sketch™ and all the mistakes disappear. Then you start over with a clean slate.

What an example of God's forgiving nature. Sure, we make mistakes — we sin. We are less than perfect — sometimes way less than perfect. But God is willing to shake those mistakes out of our lives. God is loving and forgiving. Isn't it great that even if we aren't holy, God is.

David Neil Mosser recalls a sticky situation he faced his first year of ministry. He was called to perform a funeral for one of his church members — a man who had died in prison. Even those closest to the man couldn't recall any good qualities in his life. How could Reverend Mosser preach an uplifting funeral meditation on someone whose life had been so horrible? Fortunately, one of Mosser's older colleagues gave him some good advice. He said, "Son, if you can't brag on a person ... then brag on God."[2]

Maybe we can't brag on ourselves — maybe we can't brag about our lives, but we sure can brag on God — on God's love and forgiveness. What an awesome God of mercy and grace!

So, how do we experience this forgiveness? Look at what the prodigal son did. He made the decision to come home, and that is our first step as well. We decide to return home to God.

First, we must begin by being honest with ourselves and admitting that our separation from God exists. We must come to grips with who we really are as human beings — sinners. We cannot afford the luxury of living in denial, ignoring our guilt, or hoping that our guilt will somehow magically disappear. Experiencing forgiveness is initiated through an honest confrontation with ourselves.

Second, we must remember that God is gracious and forgiving and will receive us if we will choose to humbly return. No matter how far we move away, God is there to graciously welcome us back.

Robert Robinson was an English clergyman who lived in the eighteenth century. Not only was he a gifted pastor and preacher he was also a highly gifted poet and hymn writer. However, after many years in the pastorate his faith began to drift. He left the ministry and finished up in France, indulging himself in sin.

One night he was riding in a carriage with a Parisian socialite who had recently become a Christian. She was interested in his opinion on some poetry she was reading:

> *Come thou Fount of every blessing,*
> *Tune my heart to sing thy grace,*
> *Streams of mercy never ceasing,*
> *Call for hymns of loudest praise.*

When she looked up from her reading, the socialite noticed Robinson was crying. He asked in a broken voice, "What do I think of it?" But before she could answer, he added, "I wrote it. But now I've drifted away from him and can't find my way back."

The woman responded gently, "But don't you see. The way back is written right here in the third line of your poem: *Streams of mercy never ceasing*. Those streams are flowing even here in Paris tonight."

With a reminder of God's forgiving nature that night, Robinson recommitted his life to Christ. He went home where he was embraced by God's loving arms.[3]

Do you want to experience God's forgiveness? From God's side, everything has been done — complete forgiveness is offered. From our side, some things must still be done to experience forgiveness — we must choose to return home to God. So it leaves the question ... will we? Amen.

---

1. Tom Rietveld sermon, "The Everlasting Father," found at http://pastortom.org (Advent 2000-3).

2. *The Clergy Journal* (Inver Grove Heights, Minnesota: Logos Productions, October 2002), p. 37.

3. R. Kilpatrick, "Assurance and sin," *Doubt and Assurance*, R. C. Sproul, editor (Grand Rapids, Michigan: Baker Publishing, 1993).

Six days before the Passover Jesus came to Bethany, the home of Lazarus, whom he had raised from the dead. There they gave a dinner for him. Martha served, and Lazarus was one of those at the table with him. Mary took a pound of costly perfume made of pure nard, anointed Jesus' feet, and wiped them with her hair. The house was filled with the fragrance of the perfume. But Judas Iscariot, one of his disciples (the one who was about to betray him), said, "Why was this perfume not sold for three hundred denarii and the money given to the poor?" (He said this not because he cared about the poor, but because he was a thief; he kept the common purse and used to steal what was put into it.) Jesus said, "Leave her alone. She bought it so that she might keep it for the day of my burial. You always have the poor with you, but you do not always have me."

— John 12:1-8

Experiencing Extravagant Worship

Gentlemen, imagine that you want to take your wife or girl-friend on an extravagant date. Perhaps it's a major anniversary or the right time to pop the question. At any rate, you want to show how much you love her. What would you be willing to spend? Fifty dollars or maybe even $100 a plate? And you'd probably want to give her a dozen roses, wouldn't you?[1]

Now, nothing caps off a romantic evening better than fine chocolates. The Noka Vintages Collection made in Dallas will only cost you $854 per pound — good choice. But nothing says, "I love you" like the gift of perfume. May I suggest Clive Christian's No. 1? At $2,150 an ounce it isn't cheap, but isn't she worth it?

Perhaps that all sounds a little extravagant. But aren't there times and reasons for being extravagant? Sometimes, the only way to express what we feel is by going against the ordinary and doing the extraordinary.

Babette's Feast is a Danish movie based on the book by Isak Dineson. In nineteenth-century Denmark, two spinster sisters live in an isolated seacoast village with their father, who is an honored Puritan pastor of a small Protestant church. Although they each are presented with the opportunity to marry and leave the village, the sisters choose to stay with their father — to serve both him and their church.

After their father dies, the two spinster sisters provide leadership for their small church. The group has dwindled to eleven sour-faced, pious elderly people filled with pride and suspicious of each other.

One stormy, rainy night, Babette arrives at the door of the sisters as she flees the French civil war. Drenched, exhausted, and needing sanctuary, she is a middle-aged refugee from Paris bearing a letter of recommendation from a former suitor of one of the sisters. The letter simply says, "Babette can cook."

Babette ends up staying fourteen years with the sisters, cleaning and cooking for her own room and board. Her only link to her former life is a lottery ticket that a friend in Paris renews for her every year. Then comes the exciting news that her lottery ticket has won 10,000 francs. The two sisters celebrate her good fortune but begin to grieve what they believe will be the leaving of their friend, Babette.

What Babette does next is an extravagant expression of love and gratitude. The sisters and the church had been planning a celebration of the 100-year anniversary of the birth of their founding pastor/father. Babette asks permission from the sisters to not only prepare the meal, but also to pay for it with her own money. Because Babette is Catholic, the sisters have reservations but reluctantly agree.

The church members and a few other guests gather for Babette's feast. As the cold wind howls outside, Babette treats them all to an incredible, gourmet dinner of turtle soup, caviar, quail, pastries, champagne, and rare aged wine. It is unlike anything the village has ever seen. After the feast, Babette reveals that she was once chef at a world-renowned cafe in Paris. Even more shocking is the revelation that Babette has spent her entire 10,000 francs on the feast.

At first glance, it would seem that this extravagant gift is wasted on an unappreciative pious congregation. But, that's not the way it turns out. The pious sisters and their community finally learn the true depths of faith — something which is more than just what we believe, but rather also reflects what we do and the love with which we do it. Babette's extravagant gift was one of genuine love.

In today's scripture, Mary behaves in much the same way. Mary shows us one of the most important things we need to understand if we want to draw near to the heart of Jesus. We need to learn to love him extravagantly with our whole heart.

With a heart filled with joy and thanksgiving, Mary broke the narrow neck of an alabaster jar containing a pound of pure nard and poured it on Jesus' feet. Notice it was pure nard — meaning it was very expensive. Nard could be thinned out with oil, but this was pure. This costly perfume was derived from a special plant which grew only in India. For a modern comparison, the nard would be worth about $12,300 to us. A pound of Channel No. 5 is only $2,000. Can you imagine pouring all of it on your feet? If we were to spend that much on perfume, we would want it to last a lifetime.

Why did Mary do it? It was an act of worship — an extravagant act of worship. Worship is about ascribing worth. Mary's action shows her understanding of the majesty and greatness of Jesus Christ. She shows exactly what she thinks Jesus is worth when she pours the expensive nard on his feet. She willingly, cheerfully, and eagerly gives the finest thing that she has. This is not a duty, but a delight, for her. If she had something of greater value to give, no doubt she would have given it to her Lord.

Mary's worship is selfless, sacrificial, and even extravagant. As we look at Mary's extravagant love, I hope we'll see what true worship looks like and learn to practice it in our own lives.

In contrast to Mary in the scripture is Judas Iscariot. His reaction was "What a waste!" But I challenge us to consider, would we have thought much differently?

Laura Jernigan tells of vacationing with family members one summer at a beach house. One morning, she woke up to the smell of baking bread drifting up from the kitchen. She quickly dressed, went downstairs, and found her sister-in-law in the kitchen. She was just taking a loaf of freshly baked bread out of the oven. Jernigan said hopefully, "Wow! Is this for breakfast?"

Her sister-in-law replied, "No, not this loaf. This one is for the birds."

Not understanding at all, Jernigan asked, "What?"

She repeated herself, "This one is for the birds." Then pointing to a lump of dough, she added, "The next one is for us."

Hoping that she was simply too groggy to understand, Jernigan asked for clarification, "You mean you are going to give a new loaf of bread to the birds?"

Once again her sister-in-law reiterated, "Yes, that's right."

Jernigan couldn't believe it. She thought, "What a waste of homemade bread on those noisy seagulls."

53

Her sister-in-law smiled and walked past her, heading down to the beach. Jernigan ran to the deck, convinced she was kidding. She wasn't. She got to the sand, and began tearing off hunks of the loaf and throwing them up in the air to the birds, who swooped and ate it happily.

Jernigan did get her fresh bread that morning from the second loaf — but for a long while, she couldn't get over that loaf thrown to the birds. Birds get the leftover, dried-up crusts and end-pieces of store-bought bread, not the first loaf out of the oven! She didn't get it.[2]

Judas didn't get it, either. He looked at Mary's act of extravagant worship as a waste. Then again, he wasn't worshiping Jesus — he was worshiping money. As the scripture points out, he didn't think it was a waste because he cared about the poor. He simply wanted the money for himself. The scripture says, "He was a thief; he kept the common purse and used to steal what was put into it."

Worship is about ascribing worth. Mary was showing her gratitude to Jesus for raising her brother Lazarus from the dead. What was that worth to her? Everything.

Jesus has given us the gift of life as well. The scripture asks of us the question, "What is that worth to us?" Do we respond like Mary or Judas?

One bold minister probably speaks for most of us. One Sunday after he received the offering plates from the ushers following the collection, he then held them up to the heavens, and offered this prayer of dedication, "O Lord, despite what we say, this is what we really think of you."

If we really examine ourselves this Lent, we are probably more like Judas than we want to be. We are prone to be extravagant toward ourselves but not toward others.

Michael Slaughter is the minister at Ginghamsburg UMC in Tipp City, Ohio. With a background in social work, Michael set up a ministry to connect people in his church with families needing help. The idea is to holistically help by establishing a family-to-family relationship. At Christmas, the Slaughter family had two families — their own and their adopted family.

The mother of the adoptive family was named Judy and she needed help with Christmas. While Michael and Cindy went shopping for their own family, they were buying Levi's, Adidas, and Gap. When it came time to shop for Judy's family, they went to K-Mart. Her kids were getting K-Mart clothes and K-Mart shoes.

But somewhere on the way to K-Mart, Michael said, "I'm giving the best for my family, why am I going 'discount' for Judy's family?" So they bought the same for both families — they were just as extravagant with their adoptive family as they were with their own.[3]

The gospel of Luke says it: "Where your treasure is, there your heart will be also." Mary gave extravagantly. It was obvious what she treasured — her life-giving Savior. It was just as obvious what Judas treasured — extravagance for himself.

It takes a great faith to experience extravagant worship. It takes a great faith to forget about the cost of discipleship — to completely pour out our whole heart, soul, mind, and body before our worthy Christ. Extravagant worship is holding nothing back, laying it all on the altar for him.

Showing Jesus' worth with the expensive nard was an act of extravagant faith. The Swiss psychiatrist, Paul Tournier, gave an illustration of extravagant faith. He said, "Faith is like a trapeze artist who is swinging on one bar. He is going to turn loose and grab another bar; but there's a moment after he has turned loose of the security of the second bar where he is hanging in the air with no net underneath ... The Christian life is like this — a lot of turning loose and taking hold in the living of life."[4]

How often we see people of faith at their best in the act of "turning loose." Mary turned loose of some very expensive perfume. But in the process, she grabbed hold of her Savior — she grabbed hold of what Judas couldn't grasp.

If we haven't grasped it before, I hope we grasp it this Lent. I hope we understand what our salvation is worth — everything. If we love Jesus, then we will experience extravagant worship. We will be as extravagant toward him as we are to ourselves — holding back nothing. Let us experience the extravagant worship of Jesus. Amen.

1. Prices found at Forbes.com.

2. Laura Jernigan, "Bread and Oil," *The Abingdon Preaching Annual 2004*, David N. Mosser, editor (Nashville: Abingdon Press, 2003), pp. 126-128.

3. Roger Sizemore sermon, "Learning to Splurge," found at http://www.firstchristianatlanta.com/sermon01/1apr.htm.

4. *Emphasis* (Lima, Ohio: CSS Publishing Company, Inc., 2004), March-April, p. 35.

After he had said this, he went on ahead, going up to Jerusalem.

When he had come near Bethphage and Bethany, at the place called the Mount of Olives, he sent two of the disciples, saying, "Go into the village ahead of you, and as you enter it you will find tied there a colt that has never been ridden. Untie it and bring it here. If anyone asks you, 'Why are you untying it?' Just say this, 'The Lord needs it.'" So those who were sent departed and found it as he had told them. As they were untying the colt, its owners asked them, "Why are you untying the colt?" They said, "The Lord needs it." Then they brought it to Jesus; and after throwing their cloaks on the colt, they set Jesus on it. As he rode along, people kept spreading their cloaks on the road. As he was now approaching the path down from the Mount of Olives, the whole multitude of the disciples began to praise God joyfully with a loud voice for all the deeds of power that they had seen, saying, "Blessed is the king who comes in the name of the Lord! Peace in heaven, and glory in the highest heaven!" Some of the Pharisees in the crowd said to him, "Teacher, order your disciples to stop." He answered, "I tell you, if these were silent, the stones would shout out."   — Luke 19:28-40

Passion/Palm Sunday
Luke 19:28-40

Experiencing Hope

During spring break a few years ago, my family and I went to Disney World. We tried to plot out our route through the park so we would squeeze in all the "must do" rides. We also scheduled in a Disney character parade that we felt was a "must see." All the great Disney characters ranging from Mickey Mouse to Arial the mermaid would be there.

When we told our son, Spencer, the next thing we were doing was a parade, he got excited. After all, he had been to many parades back home in Heavener — often standing on the corner of East First and C Avenue. He knew what to expect, so he wanted to get a front row seat. Based on his great knowledge, he eagerly asked, "Are they going to throw out candy?"

We had to explain to him that there would be no horses, no fire truck, no classic cars, and no candy thrown. This was a different kind of parade.

And it was a different kind of parade that took place in today's scripture from Luke — unlike anything the people had ever seen. There wasn't any candy and there wasn't even a multitude of VIPs. Just one man humbly riding on a young donkey, but his presence caused the crowd to spread their coats on the ground like a red carpet and proclaim him king. The crowd sang, "Blessed is the king who comes in the name of the Lord!"

But like I said, this was no ordinary parade — and no ordinary king. Kings of the day didn't ride into town on donkeys. In a typical processional, the king would ride a warhorse.

So what kind of king was Jesus? He was the king of tax collectors, fishermen, Samaritans, harlots, blind men, demoniacs, and cripples. Those who followed Jesus were a ragtag bunch — pathetically unfit for their grand hopes of a Jewish kingdom. They were the least, the last, and the lost — the blind, the lame, and the outcast.

These coats they threw were not fine garments — they were sweaty, dusty rags. Before Jesus came, these people in the crowd were desperate and nearly hopeless. Now Jesus was riding into Jerusalem and he brought a moment of possibility. Their last hope was riding into town on a borrowed young donkey.

Have you ever been that desperate? Have you ever felt so hopeless that you were looking for any sign that things could be better?

Bruce Larson tells about a friend who was driving through Kentucky and decided to leave the main highway to see more of the rural areas of the state. He found himself in a small town called No Hope, Kentucky. He drove around to see the town with an eye toward the churches. Sure enough, he came upon a lovely little white structure with a big sign in front that identified it as "No Hope Baptist Church."

Unfortunately, I've known too many churches of various denominations that were the No Hope Church. That's because there are so many people — including Christians — who live as if they have little or no hope.

The good news is that we don't have to live that way — King Jesus brings us hope. Even in their hopelessness, this ragtag group at the Jesus parade knew that the man on the donkey was king. They placed all their hope in him.

By riding on the young donkey, Jesus was sending an unmistakable message about his identity. One of the best-known prophecies in that day concerning the coming of the Messiah came from Zechariah:

> *Rejoice greatly, O daughter of Zion! Shout aloud, O daughter of Jerusalem! Lo, your king comes to you, triumphant and victorious is he, humble and riding on a donkey, on a colt, the foal of a donkey.*
> — Zechariah 9:9

By entering Jerusalem on that colt, Jesus was saying in no uncertain terms, "The prophecy is talking about ME! I am the Messiah. I am the Son of God — the Savior of the World!"

The Pharisees and religious leaders who were watching this triumphal entry recognized that. They knew what was going on. They knew what Jesus was claiming. And they wanted Jesus to stop the crowds from worshiping him. In essence they tell him, "Control your disciples! Only God deserves our worship. So stop those people from saying that!"

And Jesus responds by saying, "If they were quiet, the stones would shout my praise. Even a rock — or anyone as smart as a rock — knows who I am!"

The bottom line is that we who are Christians have hope. Our hope is in our Savior who has fulfilled the prophecies — Christ Jesus. We only need to be smarter than a rock to figure that out. Like the ragtag bunch gathered at that first Palm Sunday parade, we're not perfect. We know that evil pervades this world. But like those parade goers, we also know that Jesus gives us hope amidst the evil.

According to Greek mythology, a woman named Pandora was created by the gods to punish humanity. She was sent to Prometheus because he had secured fire from the gods. Knowing that she was a trap, he refused her. However, his brother, Epithemeus, gladly accepted her and fell in love with her. The two, along with the rest of humanity, had lived a life in a paradise — dancing, playing, and enjoying delicious foods.

Now, each of the gods had endowed Pandora with their own special quality, making her as attractive as possible. The most significant of these gifts was a *pithos* or storage jar, given by Zeus. It contained her dowry and over time became known as Pandora's Box. Being warned from his brother, Epimetheus told Pandora never to open the jar she had received from Zeus.

However, Pandora's curiosity got the better of her. She was no longer interested in playing and dancing in the garden. So she opened it, releasing all the misfortunes of humankind — diseases, sorrow, poverty, vices, crime, despair, and greed. They flew out in the form of horrible little moth-like creatures who mercilessly stung Pandora, Epithemeus, and their friends. People cried, and began quarrelling.

But Pandora had shut the jar before everything came out. She took the chance to open it again deciding it would be impossible to do any more harm than had already been done. Hope flew out. Having been concealed among the evil creatures by the gods, hope was now free to heal the wounds inflicted by evil.

Even amidst our modern-day evil, we know that hope is always present. In Jesus, hope wasn't just released — it was enfleshed. Hope was born in stable and raised as a man, now coming to the people. In our desperate times — in the dark night of our souls — we have a hope that endures.

Many of you will remember the Lebanese hostage situation in the mid 1980s. One of the hostages was David Jacobsen who was in Beirut as a hospital administrator. For eighteen months he endured a harsh existence of chains and blindfolds, of cold dirt floors and terrible loneliness.

He was finally released on November 2, 1986. He later told of attending a California Angels baseball game the summer following his release. He went early to take in the whole experience: studying the crowd as they drifted in, listening to the venders hawk sodas and ice cream, watching the players warm up, and tasting a steaming hot dog with extra relish and mustard.

In his mind, he had been there a million times while still chained to a wall in Beirut. In almost a prayer, his mind drifted to wonderful memories of freedom. Mentally, he attended his daughter's wedding, bounced his grandson on his knee, attended Fourth of July picnics, and drove along the California coast in his old Plymouth convertible.

Jacobsen believed he would do all these things again because he had absolute faith that God would see him through. He said, "My patriotism, my faith, and my belief in myself all grew during my ordeal. It had to." And he explained how he endured his captivity by saying, "More than anything, hope is the nourishment of survival."[1]

Where did he turn to find hope? His hope was grounded in his faith — grounded in God. Because of his hope and faith, he was able to survive a year and a half of captivity.

How do we experience this hope? Where does it come from? As the great hymn of faith says, "My hope is built on nothing less than Jesus' blood and righteousness." When you really think about those words, they seem strange to us. We may ask, "Really, our hope is found in blood? In suffering?"

As we've already pointed out, today is Palm Sunday. However, today is also designated Passion Sunday. It is a reminder that even though today is a triumphant entry, there is a seemingly not so triumphant exit at the end of the week. As we think about the death of Christ, do we naturally think, "Wow! Jesus will be tortured and crucified. Now I have hope!"? I doubt it. Yet, because of the painful bloody death of Jesus, we have hope. Because of our sin — our evil, vices, crimes, greed, and dishonesty — we have earned a death sentence. Because Jesus took on our death sentence, we have hope. Our hope lies not with the belief that Jesus came to suffer *with* his people — but that he came to suffer *for* us. He took our place in death.

This is not what those ragtag followers who gathered at the palm parade were expecting. A king who dies was not in their plans. But it is what they received. They hoped for an earthly king and received a heavenly king. They hoped for the temporal but received the eternal.

In *Christianity Today*, Gary Thomas relays that when George Bush was vice-president, he represented the US at the funeral of former Soviet leader, Leonid Brezhnev. Bush was deeply moved by a silent protest carried out by Brezhnev's widow. She stood motionless by the coffin until seconds before it was closed. Then, just as the soldiers touched the lid, Brezhnev's wife performed an act of great courage, hope, and civil disobedience: She reached down and made the sign of the cross on her husband's chest.[2]

There in the stronghold of atheistic power, the wife of one of world's most powerful faithless leaders expressed her hope that her husband was wrong. She hoped that there was another life. She expressed hope that Jesus really had fulfilled the prophecy — the hope that Jesus was the Messiah — the Son of God — the Savior of the world.

This is the hope we have in Christ: in life, in death, in life beyond death, Christ is with us. He died, so that we might live — so that we might have hope in this life and the life to come.

In the midst of all the evil and darkness that we experience in life, we know we can experience hope. Jesus comes fulfilling prophecy: Your king comes to you, triumphant and victorious is he, humble and riding on a donkey. Amen.

---

1. *Guideposts* '94 (Carmel, New York: Daily Guideposts, 1994), pp. 47-48.

2. Gary Thomas, *Christianity Today* (Carol Stream, Illinois: Christianity Today International, 1994), October 3, 1994, p. 26.

After this, when Jesus knew that all was now finished, he said (in order to fulfill the scripture), "I am thirsty." A jar full of sour wine was standing there. So they put a sponge full of the wine on a branch of hyssop and held it to his mouth. When Jesus had received the wine, he said, "It is finished." Then he bowed his head and gave up his spirit.

Since it was the day of Preparation, the Jews did not want the bodies left on the cross during the sabbath, especially because that sabbath was a day of great solemnity. So they asked Pilate to have the legs of the crucified men broken and the bodies removed. Then the soldiers came and broke the legs of the first and of the other who had been crucified with him. But when they came to Jesus and saw that he was already dead, they did not break his legs. Instead, one of the soldiers pierced his side with a spear, and at once blood and water came out. (He who saw this has testified so that you may believe. His testimony is true, and he knows that he tells the truth.) These things occurred so that the scripture might be fulfilled, "None of his bones shall be broken." And again another passage of scripture says, "They will look on the one whom they have pierced."

After these things, Joseph of Arimathea, who was a disciple of Jesus, though a secret one because of his fear of the Jews, asked Pilate to let him take away the body of Jesus. Pilate gave him permission; so he came and removed his body. Nicodemus, who had at first come to Jesus by night, also came, bringing a mixture of myrrh and aloes, weighing about a hundred pounds. They took the body of Jesus and wrapped it with the spices in the linen cloths, according to the burial custom of the Jews. Now there was a garden in the place where he was crucified, and in the garden there was a new tomb in which no one had ever been laid. And so, because it was the Jewish day of Preparation, and the tomb was nearby, they laid Jesus there.   — John 19:28-42

Experiencing Death

T.G.I.F.! Thank God It's Friday! What does it mean to you? Normally, it is a celebration that the workweek is finally over, and we can now move on to things that we enjoy — spending time with family and friends, engaging in hobbies and passions, rejuvenating, relaxing, and winding down.

For some it means partying over the weekend in the basest sense of the term. This is evidenced in the disco movie titled, *Thank God It's Friday*, from the late 1970s starring Donna Summer. The movie's tagline summed it up: "Let's blow this joint into another space zone."

More recently, R. Kelly sang the same sentiments in a song of the same title: "Thank God it's Friday — it's a party."

But the sentiments of the expression "Thank God it's Friday" carries an entirely different meaning on Good Friday. Thank God it's Friday — for this is the day Jesus died.

Almost sounds anti-Christian, doesn't it — celebrating the death of Jesus. It would sound more fitting to say, "Thank God it's Sunday!" Sure. Palm Sunday was a celebration. You remember. We celebrated hope riding into town. And we look forward to Easter Sunday. Now that's cause for celebration — the resurrection. We can get into celebrating the defeat of death.

But death itself? We don't embrace it — let alone thank God for it. Hard to think that there is anything good about it. Anyone who has lost a loved one has struggled with death — and consequently struggled with grief.

However, the scriptural reality is this: You can't get to Easter from Palm Sunday without going through the cross — without experiencing death. So here we are on Good Friday experiencing the death of Christ as we encounter John's version of the crucifixion.

What we need to remember today is that Jesus was no helpless victim here. He wasn't powerless and subjected to the whims of his enemies. No, this was the fulfillment of God's plan.

William Holman Hunt created an insightful painting of Christ, titled *The Shadow of Death*, which is housed at the Manchester City Art Gallery. The painting depicts a weary Jesus standing inside his father's carpenter shop in Nazareth. Stripped down to a white cloth around his waist, he stretches his arms above his head.

The late afternoon sun casts a shadow onto the wall behind him. The stretching shadow overlays on a long narrow horizontal tool rack hanging on the wall. As the tool rack intersects with the shadow, the resulting merger gives the impression of a crucified Jesus. A red sash near his feet lies in a circle as if it were a bloody crown of thorns.

Mary is in the foreground on the left side of the picture. She kneels among the woodchips, with her hands resting upon a chest that houses the gifts of the magi — a reminder of her son's divinity. She is obviously startled by the premonition of the cross-like shadow cast by her son.[1]

Hunt's painting shows us in art form what the gospels tell us with words. The shadow of the cross was cast over Christ's life from the beginning. This was the journey from the moment the Word was made flesh.

The scripture says every detail of his death was planned. Prophecies of his atoning death had been proclaimed and were now being fulfilled. To that end, John reports that his bones were not broken, but his side was pierced.

But why? Why the plan to die? Why was this God's plan? Jesus was a wonderful teacher. Why wasn't that his destiny? He could have taught many more years and reached so many more people with his wisdom. Why was death his calling? There must be a greater purpose in it. There must be a reason we call the day of his death good.

Barbara Brown Taylor tells of attending a retreat where the leader asked all the participants to think of someone who represented Christ in their lives. When it came time to share their answers, one woman stood up and said, "I had to think hard about that one. I kept thinking, 'Who is it who told me the truth about myself so clearly that I wanted to kill him for it?' "[2]

According to John, Jesus died because he told the truth to everyone he met. He *was* the truth — the light that exposed the darkness of humanity's sin. It was our sin that put Jesus on the cross. When we start naming those responsible for the death of Jesus, we blame the Jews and the Roman authorities, but if the truth is told, it is us. You, me, and every other sinner in the world are responsible. When the Word became flesh and walked among us, we were exposed for who we are: sinners.

The death of Christ was a response to the sin of humanity. Sin was a problem because it separated us from God. If sin is the problem, then love is the solution. Love was the way to reconnect us to God. A clue to Jesus' mission is given in his final words spoken from the cross: It is finished.

What did he mean by that statement? For John, it means Jesus has completed the task given to him — to make the Father known. The Greek verb used here, *teleo*, means "completion" or "arriving at the intended goal."

Jesus completed the full revelation of God's love. The Word made flesh — sent because "God so loved the world" — is fully human and willingly dies on a cross. Love is revealed even in the face of suffering. As a human experiencing death, Jesus reveals the fullness of God's love in a way never before possible. Out of a deep love for us, Jesus gave up what human beings hold most dear — life.

A folk story tells of the warehouse district of a town on the Mississippi River. Daily the channel had to be dredged so that the barges were able to navigate. When the sand comes up out of the bottom of the river and is dumped on the side, it creates huge sand hills which are virtually irresistible to children. As attractive as they are for play, they are just as dangerous. When the sand comes out of the river bottom, it's wet and it creates a crust on the top of the hills. The hills feel firm, but they can easily collapse. In reality, they are a mound of quicksand.

Some years ago, two brothers didn't come home for dinner, and their bikes were found outside the fence where the dredging occurred. The family as well as other rescuers began to search frantically for the two brothers.

They finally found one. He was buried up to his chin in the sand. Because of the pressure of the wet sand and muck around him he was not breathing so they began to dig frantically. When they uncovered him down to his waist he regained consciousness and the family, in hysterics, began to say, "Where's your brother? Where's your brother? Where's your brother?" And when he could finally reply, he said, "I'm standing on his shoulders."

The one brother had given his life for the benefit of the other. It was the ultimate sacrifice — the ultimate display of love. It reflects the act of Christ on the cross — an act of grace demonstrating an incomprehensible love. Jesus himself said it best: No one has greater love than this, to lay down one's life for one's friends (John 15:13).

But I wonder ... do we miss the impact of the death of Christ? Obviously the death is apparent, but do we miss the bigger picture of what Christ's death means? Why else would we struggle to experience his death as good?

When Leith Anderson was a boy, he grew up outside of New York City and was an avid fan of the old Brooklyn Dodgers. One day, his father took him to a World Series game between the Dodgers and the Yankees. He was so excited, and he just knew the Dodgers would trounce the Yankees. Unfortunately, the Dodgers never got on base, and his excitement was shattered.

Years later, he was engrossed in a conversation with a man who was a walking sports almanac. Anderson told him about the first major league game he attended and added, "It was such a disappointment. I was a Dodger fan and the Dodgers never got on base."

The man exclaimed, "You were there? You were at the game when Don Larsen pitched the first perfect game in all of World Series history?"

Anderson replied, "Yeah, but uh, we lost."

He then realized that he had been so caught up in his team's defeat that he missed out on the fact that he was a witness to a far greater page of history.[3]

When Anderson thought of that game, all he saw was defeat. There are those who see the cross and see nothing but defeat — and they miss the bigger picture. What happened on the cross was the greatest display of love that the world has ever witnessed. Christ willingly offered his life so that we might have eternal life, and when we fully understand what Christ did through the cross, it deeply impacts us for life.

Garrison Keillor, of Lake Wobegon fame, recalled his childhood Thanksgiving dinners. As his family gathered around the table and remembered the blessings of the past year, Uncle John usually gave the prayer. This would cause everyone to squirm. As Keillor said, "Everybody in the family knew that Uncle John couldn't pray without talking about the cross and crying."

Sure enough, Uncle John prayed, talked about the cross, and cried. Then Keillor adds these memorable words, "All of us knew that Jesus died on the cross for us, but Uncle John had never gotten over it."[4]

No one who understands the implication of the cross is ever going to get over it. The love of Christ is that overwhelming. And, fully experiencing his death makes that kind of an impact.

So thank God it's Friday! Thank God that we experience the death of Christ. Because within it, we experience the deep love of God — an unlimited love that knows no bounds. A love that forgives and then goes beyond this life. Good Friday calls us to reflect on Christ's gift — Christ's sacrifice. If we don't do it any other time during the year, let us reflect on that over the next two days. Amen.

---

1. http://www.manchestergalleries.org.

2. Barbara Brown Taylor, "The Perfect Mirror," *The Christian Century* (Chicago: Christian Century, 1998), p. 283.

3. Dean Register, "A Question Of Values," in *Minister's Manual, 1995*, James Cox, Richard William Cox, and James M. Cox (New York: HarperCollins, 1994), p. 339.

4. Bill Bouknight, "Standing in the Light of the Cross," in *The Good News* magazine (Milford, Ohio: United Church of God, 2002), March/April, p. 21.

If for this life only we have hoped in Christ, we are of all people most to be pitied.

But in fact Christ has been raised from the dead, the first fruits of those who have died. For since death came through a human being, the resurrection of the dead has also come through a human being; for as all die in Adam, so all will be made alive in Christ. But each in his own order: Christ the first fruits, then at his coming those who belong to Christ. Then comes the end, when he hands over the kingdom to God the Father, after he has destroyed every ruler and every authority and power. For he must reign until he has put all his enemies under his feet. The last enemy to be destroyed is death. — 1 Corinthians 15:19-26

Experiencing Everlasting Life

Brian La Croix tells of a tragic and painful childhood memory that impacted his impressions of Easter. It happened during a family trip — he doesn't recall where they were going, or how old he was because of memory loss due to the tragedy — but he vividly remembers what happened. His dad was driving down the highway that dark night when all of a sudden, a small rabbit ran across the road. There was a sickening thud as the little flop-eared fur ball met with the tires of the car. Witnessing what had just transpired; Brian cried out to his father, "You ran over the Easter Bunny!"

Brian says tongue-in-cheek, "The trauma still haunts me. I struggle with forgiving my father for that heartless, cruel act."

As he matured though, he realized that his father did not purposely run over the rabbit. And he also realized that the rabbit meeting his doom that evening wasn't really the Easter Bunny. However at the time of the incident, his feelings concerning Easter were very real. He thought that since the Easter Bunny was dead, Easter was dead. There was no hope for Easter.[1]

Imagine for just a moment that Easter was dead. Imagine that Jesus didn't rise from the dead. Imagine that Good Friday was the end of it all — that death had the final word. There would be no hope for Easter.

In the Corinthian church the resurrection came into question as some were saying there was no resurrection of the dead. So in chapter 15 of 1 Corinthians, Paul describes how necessary the resurrection is to the Christian faith. It is everything. Without it, faith is empty. Christianity would be like every other religion in the world. In fact, it would be worse because it would be making a false claim.

Lee Strobel felt Christianity was doing just that — making a false claim. As a journalist, he was an avowed atheist. Strobel earned a journalism degree from the University of Missouri and a Master of Studies in Law degree from Yale Law School. He became an award-winning legal editor of *The Chicago Tribune* and was awarded Illinois' highest honors from UPI for both investigative reporting and for public service journalism.

After his wife, Leslie, came into the faith, he used his investigative reporter skills to begin a two-year examination of the historical, scientific, and philosophical evidence for Christianity. What happened was incredible. After viewing the evidence, the award-winning atheistic journalist believed in Christ — resurrection and all.

Strobel became a minister and the *New York Times* best-selling author of nearly twenty books including *God's Outrageous Claims*, *The Case for Christ*, *The Case for Faith*, and *The Case for Easter.*

In today's scripture, the apostle Paul makes his case for Easter and the resurrection. He asserts the main claim of Easter and of Christianity: "Christ has been raised from the dead." And, Christ's resurrection has a purpose: so that "all will be made alive in Christ." Death has no hold on us any longer, as "the last enemy to be destroyed is death."

Yet how often do we ignore our basic belief and fear death? We live as if Easter was dead — as if Christ stayed in the grave. We fear death.

During a Bible study, the leader asked the group, "If you found out that you only had two weeks to live what would you do?" After a few minutes of silence, one man said, "I would quit my job, sell my possessions, and travel." Another said, "I would call all of my family and friends and plan a going-away party." A third said, "I would invite my mother-in-law to come and live with me."

A bit puzzled by the third man's answer the leader asked if he would explain. He said, "I would invite my mother-in-law to come and live with me because it would be the longest two weeks of my life!"

We fear death and want to hold onto this life — partly because we know that death has eternal consequences related to sin. Paul reminded the Corinthians that death came through Adam's disobedience.

Sin leads to death.

Comedian, W. C. Fields, who was known for being a Hollywood playboy, was allegedly on his deathbed when a friend came to visit him and was astonished to find him reading the Bible. The friend asked, "What in the world are you doing reading the Bible?" W. C. Fields said, "I'm looking for loopholes."

We know that sin leads to death — that thought can be scary. But I believe we also fear death because it is an unknown. We fear what we don't know.

Have you talked with someone who died and came back to tell you about the afterlife? There are reports of near-death experiences where people speak of a white light or a tormented feeling. But have you actually visited with someone who was resident in the afterlife? Do any of us have firsthand experience of death? We fear what we don't know.

Max Lucado, in his book, *Six Hours One Friday*, tells the story of a missionary in Brazil who discovered a tribe of Indians in a remote part of the jungle. The tribe was in need of medical attention as a contagious disease was ravaging the population. People were dying daily.

A hospital was not too terribly far away — across a large river, but the Indians would not cross it because they believed it was inhabited by evil spirits. To enter the water would mean certain death.

The missionary explained how he had crossed the river and was unharmed. They were not impressed. He then took them to the bank and placed his hand in the water. They still wouldn't go in. He walked into the water up to his waist and splashed water on his face. It didn't matter. They were still afraid to enter the river.

Finally, he dove into the river, swam beneath the surface until he emerged on the other side. He punched a triumphant fist into the air. He had entered the water and escaped. It was then that the Indians broke out into a cheer and followed him across.[2]

That's exactly what Jesus did! He took the fear out of death as he conquered it through the resurrection. Even though he had raised the dead with the touch of his hand and the call of his voice, they wouldn't believe. But when he died and was resurrected, he led the way and the people believed.

Paul calls Jesus' actions in the resurrection "firstfruits." What he is saying is that we follow Jesus in the resurrection. If Jesus is firstfruit, we are second. Just as Jesus experienced everlasting life, so do we.

Just as death came through Adam, life came through Christ. When Paul lays out his Adam-Christ argument, he wants us to see what we have in Christ — resurrection and everlasting life. The death produced by Adam is ultimately overcome in Christ.

Easter shouts to all who will listen: The enemy of death has been destroyed! Adam's disobedience leading to death has been reversed by the obedience of Christ. The resurrection is real.

- Jesus is no longer on the cross. The cross is empty.
- Jesus is no longer wrapped in grave clothes. They are empty.
- Jesus is no longer in the tomb. The tomb is empty.

Christ is risen! We are no longer quite so afraid of death. Death loses some of its power and sting.

There's a wonderful story told about a father and his seven-year-old daughter who were driving around in their car on a fresh spring day. A great big yellow bee flew into the car. The little seven-year-old girl was very much afraid — and so was the father.

They tried desperately to get the bee out of the car. But they couldn't. It just kept buzzing from the front of the car to the back — scaring them both as it flew past their heads. The little girl was starting to get hysterical and the father was shouting at her not to be afraid — which only made her more hysterical.

About that time, that great big yellow bee landed on the father's neck and stung him. The little girl became so petrified, she started crying hysterically. The father tried to calm her down and finally said to her, "You don't need to be afraid anymore. The bee has lost its sting; its stinger is right here in my neck; the bee has lost its sting."

The bee is nothing without the sting. To use Paul's words, Easter causes us to question: "Where, O death is your victory? Where,

O death is your sting?" On Easter, the sting of death was removed. The stinger is located in the neck of Jesus the Christ.

Charles Wesley wrote about it in the classic Easter hymn, "Christ The Lord Is Risen Today" (1739) — remember?

> *Lives again our glorious King,*
> *Where, O death, is now thy sting?*
> *Once he died our souls to save,*
> *Where's thy victory boasting grave?*
> *Soar we now where Christ has led,*
> *Following our exalted Head,*
> *Made like him, like him we rise,*
> *Ours the cross, the grave, the skies ...*[3]

We sing about it and I hope we believe it. Because Christ rose, so do we. Because Christ is alive, we experience everlasting life. Death doesn't have the last word. There is tomorrow.

After his mother died, a small boy was being raised by his father. Trying to be both mommy and daddy, the father had planned a picnic. The little boy had never been on a picnic and was very excited. The night before the picnic, the boy couldn't sleep. He tossed and he turned, but the excitement got to him. Finally, he got out of bed, ran into the room where his father had already fallen asleep, and shook him. His father woke up and saw his son. He said to him, "What are you doing up? What's the matter?"

The boy said, "I can't sleep."

The father asked, "Why can't you sleep?"

Answering, the boy said, "Daddy, I'm excited about tomorrow."

His father replied, "Well, son, I'm sure you are, and it's going to be a great day, but it won't be great if we don't get some sleep. So why don't you just run down the hall, get back in bed, and get a good night's rest."

So the boy trudged off down the hall to his room and got in bed. The father fell asleep, but not the son. He was soon by his father's side pushing and shoving him. His father was about to scold the boy until he saw the expression on the boy's face. The father asked, "What's the matter now?"

The boy said, "Daddy, I just want to thank you for tomorrow."

The message of Easter is so clear: We have reason to be thankful — Christ has given us a tomorrow. There is no need to fear death — Christ has destroyed that enemy. Thanks be to God who gives us the victory in our Lord, Christ Jesus!

Because of Easter, we can and will experience everlasting life. Let us experience God's love as the last word over death. Alleluia! Amen.

---

1. Bryan La Croix sermon, "Because He Lives ..." sermoncentral.com.

2. Max Lucado, *Six Hours One Friday* (Nashville: Thomas Nelson Publishers, 1989), p. 157.

3. "Christ The Lord Is Risen Today," words by Charles Wesley, 1739, in the public domain.